The enchanter Merlin, magician of King Arthur's Round Table

Satan (Pluto) holding court for newly anointed witches. From Gerard d'Euphrates' *Livre de l'histoire & ancienne cronique*, printed by E. Groulleau, Paris, 1549.

Modern Witchcraft Spellbook

by
Anna Riva

Author of

Prayer Book
Powers of The Psalms
Candle Burning Magic
Devotions to The Saints
Secrets of Magical Seals
The Modern Herbal Spellbook
Modern Witchcraft Spellbook
Golden Secrets of Mystic Oils
Magic With Incense and Powders
Spellcraft, Hexcraft & Witchcraft
Voodoo Handbook of Cult Secrets
Your Lucky Number ... Forever

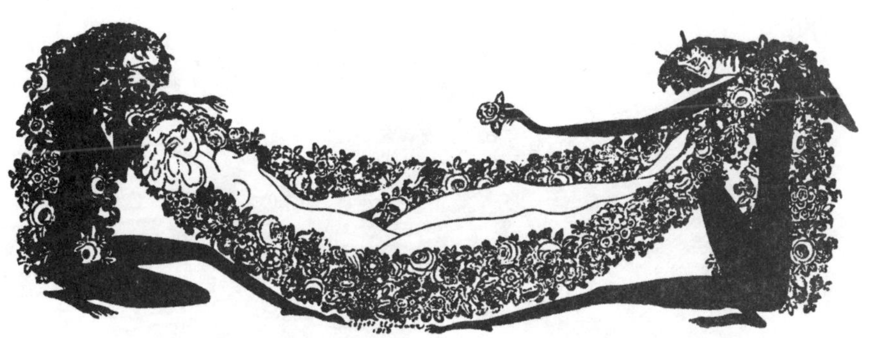

INTERNATIONAL IMPORTS
236 W. MANCHESTER AVE,
LOS ANGELES, CA 90003

Reprint 1993

Occult Books - Curios - Supplies

ISBN 0-9438-3202-0

The Dice-Demon tempting the gambler. Detail from a broadside warning against dice-playing, France, 1490.

CONTENTS

SPELL RITUALS

ROOT AND HERB RITUALS

Sorcerer riding the waves on a piece of flotsam.
From Olaus Magnus' *Historia de gentibus septentrionalibus,* Rome, 1555.

Sorcerer selling a bag of wind (tied up in three knots of a rope).

SPELLS

A spell is a word, a formula, or a ritual which is supposed to have magical powers. It is an "instant miracle." It is a way to accomplish your objectives without work, study, or delay. There are few of us who can resist such a simple solution to our most vexing situations.

For every situation occult authors have invented a spell to solve the problem or to attain the goal. This volume covers nineteen of these varied objectives, from getting and holding a job to winning back a lover who has left home.

As in all belief, the power of suggestion is the most potent ingredient. As in all remedies, the force of positive thinking is the great healer. And as in all magic, it is the magical powers of the mind which accomplish true sorcery.

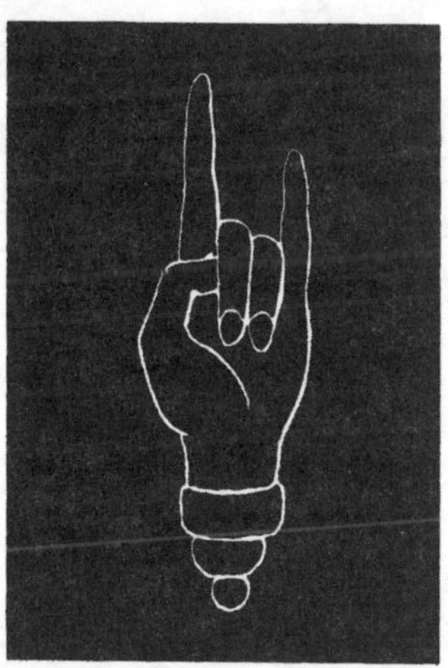

The legendary spells in this book are compiled from ancient folklore, various occult writings, regional superstition, and other mystical sources. It is given as curiosa only, and no claims of supernatural powers are made for any ritual or materials, and no guarantees are offered nor implied. Neither the author nor publisher assume any responsibility for the outcome from the use of any of these rituals, materials, or ingredients.

De lanijs et phitonicis mu-
lieribus ad illustrissimum principem dominū Sigismūdum
archiducem austrie tractatus pulcherrimus

Witches brewing up a hailstorm. From the title page of Ulrich Molitor's *De lanijs et phitonicis mulieribus,* printed by Cornelius de Zierikzee, Cologne, 1489.

TO ATTRACT THE LOVE OF THE OPPOSITE SEX

Romantic spells should always begin when the moon is waxing, and the Venus hours are most conducive to love and lovers. Be guided by these planetary hours and arrange your actions and encounters accordingly.

Sunday	2:00 and 9:00 AM	4:00 and 11:00 PM
Monday	6:00 AM	1:00 and 8:00 PM
Tuesday	3:00 and 10:00 AM	5:00 and 12:00 PM
Wednesday	7:00 AM	2:00 and 9:00 PM
Thursday	4:00 and 11:00 AM	6:00 PM
Friday	1:00 and 8:00 AM	3:00 and 11:00 PM
Saturday	5:00 AM and Noon	7:00 PM

Always sprinkle your clothes and skin with Love Powder before going out to meet any person of the opposite sex. When you bathe each day, use two spoonsful of Love Bath in the water.

A letter should be written to the person you wish to attract, for one must be aware of your feelings before they can respond favorably. Anoint the letter with Love Drops or Magnet Oil before sending it. Either of these oils can also be used as a perfume, and should be applied particularly to the inside of the elbows and back of the ears.

Use Attraction Incense to keep your home alight with the proper vibrations, and remember to burn this at the Venus hour. While the incense is burning, read Psalm 138 which is an aid to love and friendship.

Many herbs are used in love philters, and one of the most potent and aromatic is lavender. Place a bit of this in the drawer where your most intimate clothes are stored, or in your linen closet amongst the sheets you use on the bed.

A Seal of Special Attraction should be carried with you, and the name of the person you wish to attract is to be written on the back.

The gods smile on those who seek love cheerfully, so make your surroundings as well as yourself attractive and pleasing. Keep your actions and thoughts on a high place, remembering always that a smile and a friendly word attracts a pleasant reply.

May each day be a little better than the one before.

SO BE IT...

Other traditional love charms and talismans . . .

Queen's Root can be carried by those who wish to be attractive to the opposite sex.

Lovage Root is worn near the heart to attract a lover.

The Seal of Love is designed for gaining and holding the love of another.

A piece of rose quartz is carried for love, fidelity, peace, and a happy marriage.

Pronounce three times your own name and the name of the one you love. Then take off all your clothes and slip into the room where the lover lies sleeping soundly. Clip from the loved one's head a lock of hair. If you do this without awakening the sleeping person, you will obtain absolute mastery over their affections. Wear the hair in a bag around your neck. If you are caught or observed during this spell, it will turn against you and you will suffer a lack of affection from the one you wished to attract.

Make a figure of clay in the shape of the one you love, mixing with the clay some of your own saliva. Bury the image beneath a place where the beloved will surely pass, and the lover will suffer great torments if your love is not returned.

Get two red image candles (one male and one female) and anoint both with Love Drops or Lovers Oil. Write your own name on the back of the appropriate candle, using a new nail, and the name of the one you desire on the back of the other candle. Place the candles facing each other, and burn them both for an hour. Repeat this daily until the candles are gone and your loved one will be under your spell.

Toss pieces of Ladies' Thumb herb into the path of someone you desire and they will soon be yours alone.

TO BRING PEACE BETWEEN LOVERS

One of the most tragic of life's experiences is that in which two persons love each other but influences are such that there are quarrels, arguments, and turmoil when there should be tranquility and contentment. Solutions are not easy, simple, or quick, but one must endeavor to do one's part toward settling differences in a calm, controlled, and friendly manner.

Do not heap anger upon ire. Do not give wrath in return for rage. Do not speak bitterness in reply to animosity. Do not threaten when faced with meanness. In spite of all temptation, be gentle and quiet, bear nothing but good will toward the other person, and hold charity and forgiveness in your heart.

The manner in which you conduct yourself is a powerful force in settling disagreements. For this reason a purification bath is the first step toward achieving an amiable solution to the problems confronting you. Take a tablespoon of hyssop or lovage and soak it in one quart of water for 24 hours. Then strain, add some of this water to your bath each day for seven consecutive days.

Should you be able to see the person with whom you have quarreled, go and speak to this person, with quiet soft words and in a pleasant manner. When you go, sprinkle your body with Has No Hanna Oil or Perfume so that your promises will ring true in the ears of the one to whom you speak. If you cannot go personally to visit this lover or friend, write a letter of love and forgiveness, and sprinkle it with Has No Hanna before it is sent.

In the home, burn only Helping Hand or John the Conqueror Incense to encourage the vibrations of understanding and calm, clear thinking to prevail.

Each evening for three consecutive evenings burn a red candle. Under the candle, so that the melted wax can fall upon this paper, place a square of parchment on which you have written the name of your love nine times. While the candle is burning, read Psalms 45 and 46 which are said to possess the virtue of making peace between man and woman.

Carry with you at all times a Seal of Mars as shown in the Sixth and Seventh Books of Moses which is reputed to bring good luck in case of quarrels to all who own it.

The fires of love should be rekindled and burn again, the argument or quarrel forgotten, and all hurts between you forgiven. Let your love shine in your smile at all times and no ill-wind will quench the flame.

SO BE IT. . . . .

Other love charms which may be used . . . .

Magnolia leaves spread beneath the mattress are said to make the most frigid couple passionate.

Sprinkle violets in the corners of your home to entice the good spirits to enter and bring many blessings.

Sprinkle Anger Powder around a room to overcome feelings of irritation and anger. Helps avert fights and cleanse the mind of all evil thoughts.

To bring peace and harmony to any relationship, sprinkle Peace Powder on the head of the other person. Prevents future strife from erupting.

Burn Peace Incense to dispel the most serious of arguments and bring happiness to a rocky marriage.

To keep love between a man and wife, gather seven sticks, three for the woman and four for the man. Tie the three sticks together along with some vervain and a piece of the wife's clothing. With the four sticks, add a bit of St. John's Wort and a piece of his clothing. Add a few hairs from each head to the parcels, and then tie everything up together. Wrap the tokens in clean white paper or cloth and keep it in a special secret place where it is safe. So long as it is not lost, the marriage will endure.

TO CHANGE BAD LUCK TO GOOD

The power to better your luck, your life, and yourself lies within you and your thoughts must be kept positive and optimistic.

Remember that all fortune resulting from the employment of spells or charms should be shared with the poor. If you fail to do this, ill fortune will surely plague you again later.

On the first Thursday of a new moon, write these words on a square of parchment—Non Licet ponare in egarbona quia pretium sanguinis. Then fold the parchment ends toward the center so that the writing is concealed, and tie the parchment square with a piece of black yarn, thread, or ribbon. Carry this talisman in your pocket as a secret possession. No one must know you are wearing this talisman, and no one will understand why you are so lucky at games of chance.

Whenever you leave your home, anoint your finger tips with John the Conqueror or Magnet Oil. Either of these are good for controlling and conquering problems, and for attracting money, customers, and luck.

In your bath water, add two spoonsful of High Conquering Bath, and use this potent additive each day for seven consecutive days.

Use only Helping Hand or Lucky Planet incense in your home, and burn this at the Jupiter evening hours each day. The hours are 8 PM Sunday, 5 PM or Midnight Monday, 9 PM Tuesday, 6 PM Wednesday, 3 or 10 PM Thursday, 9 PM Friday, and 4 or 11 PM Saturday.

Memorize the 23rd Psalm, and repeat this daily to yourself. Then pray, as you feel in your own heart, or something similar to the following: "Because God is with me, I can do whatever I will. Because You are helping me, I cannot fail. Because I am strong enough to accomplish my aims, I can. Because I can do it, I will. Because I am asking in Your name, I cannot fail. I put my hand, my head, and my heart in Your hands, Lord, and I will be Thy servant."

Carry with you at all times a magnetic lodestone, around which you have wrapped a Seal of Spiritual Assistance and tied with red yarn, thread, or ribbon.

SO BE IT. . . . .

Additional charms which may be used for luck . . . .

Rose buds and petals tossed into an open fire insure good luck.

The gemstone, Chalcedony, is reputed to give the body power and those who carry it will make a fortune.

Sumbul root, carried near the heart, attracts good luck and wards off diseases.

Some peony in purse or mojo bag draws good luck in all matters.

Rub some Algiers Powder on the body to attract love and gambling luck.

Those who believe in the powers of candle burning, use green candles for financial gain, and yellow or brown ones to attract money. Many write the amount of money they need on a piece of paper and place this paper underneath the candle before it is lighted.

A Mojo Wishing Bean carried around in a red flannel bag is said to make all wishes come true.

Take a Jezebel Root and cover it with wax from a green candle and then bury it. This is said to make others spend or give away their money.

Keep seven Job's Tears under the pillow for luck. The number should be always seven for best results. The power is gone if more or less are used.

Carry some clover in a red flannel pouch and good luck will follow wherever you go.

Alfalfa protects its owner against proverty. This can be carried on the person or placed in a cupboard of the home.

TO CONQUER THOSE WHO MAKE YOU SUFFER

Untold amounts of mental and material torture may be inflicted upon one by the evil spell cast out by another with ill intentions. When you are sure of the ones who have harmed you, it may be justified to reverse unto them the evil spirits they have cast upon you and to render them helpless to again hurt you or others who may have fallen victim to their vile doings. The spirit of revenge is not one to trifle with and should only be used as a gesture of self-defense that will protect you from harm and return to the doer the same agony that they have bestowed upon you so that it will serve as a lesson to them.

Begin the spell on an evening when there is no moon, and do not let anyone see you or know of your endeavors. Take some War Powder and sprinkle it in front of the house where your enemy lives so that he or she may walk in it or step over it as they come and go from the house.

After sprinkling the War Powder, wait three days. Inside your own home, you shall burn some Helping Hand or John the Conqueror Incense each day from the first day. Each evening, light a black candle and under the candle place a piece of parchment upon which you have written the name of your enemy nine times in Dragon's Blood Ink.

On the fourth day, take a small bottle of War Water to the home of your enemy. With it, make a cross in front of the house and walk away without looking back. As you return home, sprinkle Confusion Powder so that the evil spirits who have been hounding you will be confused and go back where they came from.

On the first day of the spell ritual, scrub your floors with water to which you have added ten drops of Van Van Floor Wash. Do this every third day for two weeks as evil spirits cannot abide a place where this wash is used regularly.

For any crossed condition and to overcome enemies who plot against you, pray Psalm 7 early each morning and you will find that your enemies will cease their persecutions and leave you undisturbed.

Do these things faithfully according to instructions and you will get your satisfaction and be avenged. No longer will you be worrying when you should be enjoying peace. No longer will there be tears of anguish but they will be replaced with smiles of joy. No longer will you endure stress and strain but the gods of contentment and happiness will surround you and your home.

SO BE IT. . . . .

TO CROSS ENEMIES

When you have been sorely tried by one who deliberately wishes to harm you, and your patience has come to an end, you may wish to heap hatred on your enemy's head and have their power taken away so that any attempts they make toward injuring you will be successful no longer.

It is written that you shall take some Four Thieves Vinegar, pour it into a shallow plate, and dip into it a sheet of parchment paper. When the paper is soaked, take it out and lay it in a safe place until it is dry. Then write upon this paper the name of your enemy with Dove's Blood Ink.

Light a black candle, and as you light the candle, say the words:

> "Here stand mine enemy, all alone. He (or she) is without friend, without help. (Insert enemy's name), I pity thee. Nought is before thee, nought is behind thee. Frustration is at hand for thee. All your plans are as nought. Sickness, doubt, fear, and worry are creeping in on thee. Anger, discord, and trouble are to be thy new companions. Soon you will pay for tormenting me."

Hold the parchment in the flame of the candle which has been anointed with Black Arts Oil until every bit of the paper has burned to ashes. Then take the ashes and sprinkle them in front of your enemy's house after sundown.

Another method of using the Four Thieves Vinegar to defeat an enemy is to put a small amount in a bottle together with the enemy's name written on parchment paper. Then throw the sealed bottle into the moving water of a stream or river. This is alleged to draw the enemy with it in the sense that he or she would want to move from their present abode.

After sprinkling the ashes of parchment in front of your enemy's residence, let three days pass, and on the third night, take the War Water and sprinkle it in front of the house of your adversary. This you do as you pass by, making sure no one will see you in this act.

In your own home, you will burn some John the Conqueror or Domination Incense each day, and on the outside of your house, on all four sides, you shall sprinkle Peace Powder.

Upon arising each morning, read Psalm 70 for succor and encouragment.

Psalm 70
Make haste, O God, to deliver me, make haste to help me, O Lord.
Let them be ashamed and confounded that seek after my soul; let them be turned backward, and put to confusion, that desire my hurt.
Let them be turned back for a reward of their shame that say, Aha, aha.
Let all those that seek thee rejoice and be glad in thee; and let such as love thy salvation say continually, Let God be magnified.
But I am poor and needy; make haste unto me, O God. Thou art my help and my deliverer; O Lord, make no tarrying.

You will do all these things so that you may control your enemies and render them powerless to harm you. May you have peace and comfort from your foes, and pray there will be no sting in their tongues and no threat from their house toward you and your loved ones.

SO BE IT......................................

Other legends connected with hexing foes ....

Take a brown candle. Put some sugar in a bowl, set the candle in it, and burn it before you go to bed. Then, take what is left and throw it into your enemy's yard.

Sulphur is burned by many people believing in black magic to break spells they believe have been cast on them.

To hurt anyone, man or woman, write their full name on a piece of virgin parchment, and fold it in two. Saying the name aloud, recite three times the fate you wish them to suffer. Then cast the paper into a roaring fire.

To bewitch another, take a black feather and bury it in the southwest corner of your enemy's yard.

Make an image of your foe in wax or clay. Then take a knife and engrave the enemy's initials on it. With your hand strike the image a blow to the part of the body you wish to harm, and the corresponding member of your foe will suffer.

TO GAIN AND DEVELOP HAPPINESS

It is important to understand and to accept that a certain amount of sacrifice is necessary in your journey through life, and happiness and contentment will be attained to the highest degree by the way you withstand the pains and sufferings of the mind and body.

For strength at any time you feel depressed or rejected, repeat this short prayer,

> King of Kings and Lord of Lords, withdraw not from me this day. Let my efforts be successful and bless the work of my hands. Remove all spiritual blindness and into Thy hands I commend myself and all mankind. Amen.

After your morning bath, apply Attraction Powder to your body, and anoint your forehead with Magnet Oil or Lucky Nine Mixture. A bit of Maiden Hair secreted near the heart is said to add to the grace, beauty, and loveliness in general. Or a few Rose Buds or petals near the bosom may attract the self-confidence one needs to captivate the interest of those we approach during the day's endeavors.

In a small bag, carry with you at all times a Seal of Orion as this talisman is an assist in having one's wishes fulfilled.

Happiness comes from within, not from without, and material possessions do not bring a contented and harmonious life. Envy, jealousy, and hatred must be erased from your thoughts, and your tongue must be stilled of all words except those of kindness and purity. The heart that is heavy with bitterness or spite will never be one of joy and delight. As an aid to the proper attitude, repeat Psalm 65 each morning upon arising and each evening just before retiring.

Use only Helping Hand Incense in the home and ignite it each evening for seven nights, preferably at the Sun hours which are:

Sunday	10:00 PM	Thursday	5:00 PM
Monday	7:00 PM	Friday	9:00 PM
Tuesday	11:00 PM	Saturday	6:00 PM
Wednesday	8:00 PM		

The vibrations set up by this incense are allegedly to control any evil spirits which may be surrounding your person or your home.

After the incense is lit, light a pink or gold candle and say, "Happiness is attracted to me as a moth is attracted to flame. This attraction is so great it cannot be resisted. It draws, it pulls, it swings toward me and advances. It is mine to own." Repeat this slowly at least three times, and then extinguish the candle. Repeat the ritual for seven consecutive evenings.

You will want to bring happiness not just for yourself but to your entire household, and the Square of Saturn is very helpful. Fill in a small square of paper, preferably parchment, as shown below. Begin with number 1 and end with 9. As you work on this, chant "Hertha, bless this house and all who live it in."

4	9	2
3	5	7
8	1	6

On the reverse side of the paper, draw a very simple outline of your home and encircle it with three circles, drawn clockwise and beginning with the outermost circle. Repeat the chant with each circle.

Happiness is not dependent upon the condition in which we live, but is always the result of a good conscience, good health, a satisfying occupation, and freedom in all just pursuits.

SO BE IT. . . . .

Other charms, amulets and talismans designed for happiness and good fortune . . . .

Carry a carnelian for good health, long life, and good fortune.

A jasper is a talisman for relief from pain and for good luck.

Sapphires are worn or carried to promote peace and happiness between lovers.

Magnet Oil used as a perfume is believed to magnetize others toward you.

TO GAIN SPIRITUAL STRENGTH and RECEIVE HOLY BLESSINGS

Spiritual strength comes from within ourselves with the help of God. Holy blessings can only be received by those prepared for these gifts. So put from your heart all malice, deceit, viciousness, and evil thoughts. Take into your heart only what is pure and good and uplifting.

Each evening you should nourish your faith with meditation and sacred reading. Find a quiet place, and light a pure white candle. Then, while it is burning, read the 29th Psalm either from your Holy Bible or as written here.

Praise the Lord, you gods, praise his glory and power.
Praise the Lord's glorious name,
Bow down before the Holy one when he appears.
The Lord's voice is heard on the seas; the glorious God thunders, and his voice echoes over the ocean.
The Lord's voice is heard in all its might and majesty.
The Lord's voice breaks the cedars, even the cedars of Lebanon.
He causes the mountains of Lebanon to jump like calves, and Mount Hermon to leap like a young bull.
The Lord's voice makes the lightning flash.
His voice makes the desert shake; He shakes the desert of Kadesh.
The Lord's voice makes the deer give birth, and leaves the trees stripped bare,
While in his temple all shout, "Glory to God."
The Lord rules over the deep water; He rules as a king forever.
The Lord gives strength to his people, and blesses them with peace.

This Psalm can be repeated over and over until the candle is burned, or the time can be spent in silent prayer or meditation.

If one is seeking to find meaning in dreams or visions, a Seal of Knowledge should be worn while in bed, or placed under the pillow while one sleeps. This should make the dreams clearer and better understood.

During the day hours, carry with you the Seal of Spirits from the Sixth and Seventh Books of Moses which is to encourage the spirits to serve you in all things and fulfill all desires.

Each morning, upon arising, ask for God's assistance by saying "Dear Lord, Please help me this day in all that I try to do."

During this ritual, which should continue for seven consecutive days, use only Buddha Oil as a perfume.

God is bound to act, to pour Himself into thee as soon as He shall find thee ready. He wants only one thing from you—to find your innermost heart clean and ready for Him to accomplish his divine purpose therein. He cannot work against your will.

SO BE IT. . . . .

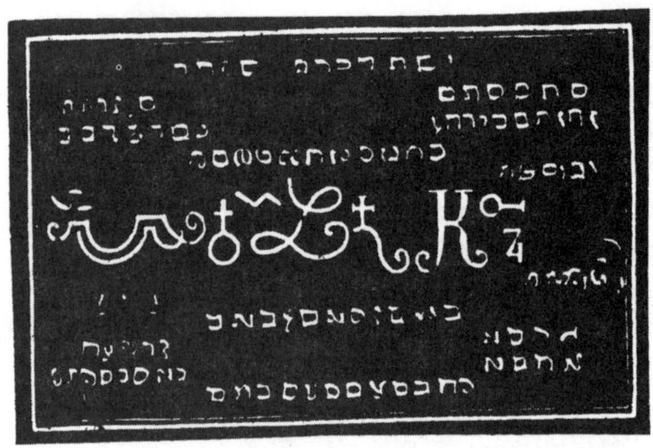

SEAL OF KNOWLEDGE

SEAL OF SPIRITS

FOR GAMBLING LUCK

So many factors affect and influence games of chance that one should attempt to bring lucky vibrations into their own individual sphere by several methods.

Certain days are reputed to be more favorable for different persons, so it may be well to engage in games on these days only –

If you were born under the sign of:	Play on:
Capricorn or Leo	Monday
Cancer or Taurus	Tuesday
Pisces or Virgo	Wednesday
Libra or Aries	Thursday
Sagittarius or Aquarius	Friday
Scorpio or Gemini	Saturday

Before playing any game of chance, sprinkle your hands with Drawing Powder and rub it in well.

Carry with you at all times, but do not let anyone else see it or touch it, a small bag—any kind will do but leather, chamois, or red flannel is said to be most powerful—in which you have a magnetic horseshoe, a magnetic lodestone, a nutmeg of India, a Seal of Good Luck and Fortune or a Seal of Honor and Wealth. To these things you may wish to add any other personal charms or talismans which you possess and which have proved their worth. You shall sprinkle the outside of the bag with three drops of Jockey Club Oil or Perfume once every week and on your particular lucky day.

As with days, everyone has certain numbers which are best suited for the date he or she was born. One may wish to memorize his own numbers and be guided by them.

BIRTHDATE:	LUCKY NUMBERS:						
Jan. 20 to Feb. 18	455	932	852	112	181	391	644
Feb. 19 to Mar. 20	744	666	810	507	531	317	216
Mar. 21 to April 18	2	179	51	81	551	995	791
April 19 to May 19	781	210	731	941	517	454	542
May 20 to June 20	900	492	611	607	339	10	843
June 21 to July 21	893	177	782	254	100	841	805
July 22 to Aug. 21	478	689	232	44	324	555	316
Aug. 22 to Sept. 22	756	409	210	455	806	903	568
Sept. 23 to Oct. 22	459	742	600	911	725	264	170

Oct. 23 to Nov. 21	325	579	563	610	908	5	167
Nov. 22 to Dec. 20	395	693	239	315	397	27	246
Dec. 21 to Jan. 19	989	12	191	918	410	914	367

Each morning, before the sun rises, repeat Psalm 4 three times. Be of good spirit always, and may the high cards and lucky numbers come your way often.

SO BE IT. . . . .

Other charms considered to be lucky . . . .

A buckeye carried in the pocket is believed to bring luck and ward off rheumatism.

Many oils are used when a change of luck is needed. Some persons rub the oils on their lodestone while others rub their hands with the perfumes. A few of the most popular gambling oils are Cleo May, Lucky John the Conqueror, Anise, Fast Luck, and Magnet.

Voodooists believe in the "gambling sack." Take a small red flannel bag and in it place a paper on which you have written the amount of money you need to win. Add a tiny stone or pebble found in a cemetery. Sew the top of the bag closed with white cotton thread. Wear this bag in the left shoe while gambling. The bag's power is restored by anointing it with Lucky John the Conqueror Oil every seventh day.

If you intend to gamble with dice, carry a John the Conqueror Root in your back pocket next to your wallet. Place your thumb on the root while you toss the dice and call out the numbers you wish to come up on each throw. This method is said to be extremely effective.

When playing cards, a bat's heart should be worn inside the sleeve of one's shuffling hand.

Burn John the Conqueror Incense before everyone arrives whenever games are played at your home.

TO GET AND HOLD A JOB

Each day use freely of God's water which you will find plentiful in your home faucet in the form of a bath to which you will pour nine drops of Oil of Rosemary for the purpose of cleansing your body so that no odor but fresh sweet scent will remain.

It is the strong in spirit and the fearless of heart who attain the blessing of God, so do not despair. Make the necessary applications for work, and do not stop after the first attempt, but keep on, and the good spirits will help you most of the way. When you obtain a job, apply yourself fully to your work and give of your best to the employer. Let no frown appear on your face as this tends to draw the spirit of evil, making it difficult for the favorable and beneficial spirits to do their work.

Good and evil are always working, and in order to fortify oneself so that the good will triumph, it is advised that we rid our minds of fear which is the foe of us all. Sit quietly in contemplation, thinking hard of fear dispelling and self-confidence growing. After a few minutes, repeat the following:

I was afraid and alone, or so I felt.
Fear I knew.
I was without heart, for weak was I,
Down in the darkness without knowledge.
Fear I knew.
Yet the time has come,
For all fear has fled.
Lightness is the word, and laughter the sword,
To fill my heart and grasp upon.
No fear I know, no doubt, no woe.
With strength, and joy, with gladness in my heart,
That fear I knew is far behind me now.
Forward the light; no dark about,
No fright, no fear in sight.
I am The One and all toward me look
And see—I have no fear.

In your home, burn only John the Conqueror Incense and before you leave the house to look for work or go to your job, anoint your forehead with Lucky Nine Mixture.

Carry with you in your pocket, or close to your person, a small bag in which you have a Seal of Relief from Want and a Southern John the Conqueror Root which is claimed to be a "helping hand" to success. Also include in your bag the stone called sardonyx which is said to help toward fame and rewards, to sharpen the wits of the owner, and to render him or her fearless and victorious.

At bedtime repeat the following prayer in a sincere manner, "Oh great and living God, who hast created man to enjoy felicity in this life, who has adopted all things for his necessity and didst declare that everything should be made subject to his will, be favorable to this prayer. Permit not the evil spirits to be in possession of my body and soul. Grant me, oh God, the power to dispose of them through your help and I will forever remain thy faithful and obedient servant."

If you have been unlucky hitherto, in spite of all efforts you sincerely made, then pray Psalm 3 each morning for nine days before the rising of the sun.

SO BE IT. . . . .

SEAL OF RELIEF FROM WANT

TO GET RID OF EVIL INFLUENCES

The most powerful of all the seals in the Sixth and Seventh Books of Moses is the Great Pentagram Seal which is designed as a protection from Black Magic, and one of these should be carried with you at all times. The Seal of Mars is also a protection against dangerous enemies and should be secreted over or near the doorway to one's home so that evil influences will not enter.

Since the 13th century, this spell has been used to drive away demons and evil spirits. They will be forced to leave you alone if you always have with you a square of parchment on which you have written these letters in this order and in this arrangment:

S	D	P	N	Q	C	N
	D	P	N	Q	C	N
		P	N	Q	C	N
			N	Q	C	N
				Q	C	N
					C	N
						N

Sprinkle a bit of Jinx Removing Salt or Powder around the outside of your home at midnight, making sure that no one sees you do this. The next morning early, wash or sweep it away thoroughly.

Before retiring at night, kneel down and repeat:

"My house has four corners. Four angels adorn it, Luke, Mark, John and Matthew.
Neither witches nor charms, nor evil-doing man must harm me, understand.
In the name of the Father, and the Son, and of the Holy Ghost. Amen."

Use only Jinx Removing Incense in the home for ten consecutive evenings, and burn this at the Mars hour which is the hour of defense.

Sunday	9:00 PM	Wednesday	7:00 PM
Monday	6:00 PM	Thursday	11:00 PM
Tuesday	10:00 PM	Friday	8:00 PM

Saturday 5:00 PM or Midnight

In your daily bath, for seven consecutive days, use two spoonsful of Jinx Removing or Uncrossing Bath, or apply Protection Oil or Rose of Crucifixion Oil to the body afterwards.

Psalms 11 and 12 should be helpful if read each day faithfully and reverently. You yourself must put forth a sincere and genuine effort to make one new friend each day, and to rid your life of all disagreeable persons around you.

SO BE IT. . . . .

Additional charms which may be used . . . .

From medieval witchcraft comes the legend of a jasper stone. This stone is used as an amulet against the trickery of witchcraft and the curse of the Evil Eye. It should be wrapped in parchment and carried in a pouch, or hung on a cord about the neck.

A Seal of Power is said to confer magical powers to those who carry it.

Devil's Bit worn about the neck is for driving evil spirits away.

The Holy Cross of Tenerife can be worn or carried for protection against evil.

HOLY CROSS OF TENERIFE

TO GET UNCROSSED

When you feel that you are crossed or cursed by the Evil Eye, it is decreed that you shall make every effort to bring peace, love, confidence, goodwill, and happiness back into your life by your own will power.

On the first day of the ritual, place some bits of Sea Lettuce in a glass of fresh water, along with ten drops of Uncrossing Oil, and set this in a window for three days. If you cannot obtain Sea Lettuce, some Mullein Herb can be just as suitable. On the fourth day, sprinkle this water in every corner of your home, making sure that no one sees you doing this.

For seven consecutive days add two spoonsful of Uncrossing or Jinx Removing Bath to the water in which you bathe. After the bath, rub Uncrossing Oil on your arms, legs, and chest and sprinkle a bit of Uncrossing Powder in your socks or shoes.

If you feel that someone has cast a spell against you in the form of an image, a legendary protective chant to be said over and over is this—"Those who have made images of me, reproducing my features, who have taken away my breath, torn my hairs, who have rent my clothes, and have stopped my feet from treading the dust; may the fire god, the almighty one, break their charm." Memorize this, and repeat it when you first awake in the morning and just before bed at night as well as often during the day.

If you know the person who is trying to harm you, cut out of paper a silhouette of a human figure and write the name of this person on the paper. It does not matter how crude the figure turns out to be, but you should do the cutting and labeling yourself. Then, each day, tear off a piece of the paper doll you have made, repeating these words as you perform the ritual—

> "Arise, O Damballah! O victim, you are seized, you are changed. Your hands become stilled, your legs bend, your back hunches, your neck twists, your teeth fall out, and your loins fester. O victim, release your sufferer or you the martyr will be."

In from five to fifteen days, this person will probably have moved away, disappeared, or turned their attention completely away from you to leave you in peace.

John the Conqueror Incense should be burned daily for seven consecutive days as this clears the air of unfavorable vibrations and allows friendly spirits to enter the room.

Psalm 7, if read in the right spirit, will help render your enemies powerless over you. A Seal of Mephistophilis, designed for conquering enemies, should be carried on your person at all times.

You, yourself, must act and speak in a cheerful and righteous way. The spirit of evil will lose all its strength to work against you, and there will be peace and tranquility in and around you and your abode.

SO BE IT...

Other traditional charms and talismans . . . .

Marjoram is prized as a charm against witchcraft, for one who is in league with the devil cannot abide the odor.

A carnelian, called the Wish Stone, is highly favorable to good health, long life, and good fortune.

Carry a Lucky Hand Root in a red flanned bag, and all hexes will be turned against their originator.

Mistletoe keeps evil away from the wearer.

Brew a tea from Poke Root and use the water to wash the doorways of your home. Do this during a new moon to break a hex.

Clover, soaked in vinegar for seven days and then sprinkled in all four corners of each room in the house, rids a home of all evil spirits.

A small bag of Five Finger Grass can be hung over the bed to ward off all witchcraft. Or make a tea of it and wash the hands and forehead with it nine times to wash away any hexes or curses there may be upon you.

Confusion Powder, when used on the forearms, breaks most curses and spells.

TO INFLUENCE OTHERS

Keep in mind that the humblest of us exerts some influence upon others, and that influence should be for good rather than evil.

Seven times each day, between 7:00 AM and 7:00 PM, read the 47th Psalm reverently. This is preferably done on the odd-numbered hours of 7, 9, 11, 1, 3, 5, and 7.

Carry with you at all times a Seal of Influence and Power which you should anoint with a drop or two of Attraction Oil. This same Attraction Oil may be used as a perfume, rubbing into the inside of your wrists and elbows before going out.

If there is a certain person you wish to dominate, the puppet spell has many advantages. Choose a Thursday when the moon is waxing, and at 8:00 AM, 3:00 PM, or 10:00 PM, and only after securing your privacy so that no one will see or hear you, take an image and label it with the name of the person you wish to sway to your will. You can use a doll, a photograph, or even a blank piece of paper cut to resemble a human figure. If you have a possession of the person you are attempting to influence, so much the better—attach hair snips with glue, rub in nail clippings, tie or sew on a sock, handkerchief, or anything belonging to the one for whom the image is made. Hold the doll or image in your two hands in front of you, concentrate on the person involved, and chant, at least seven times—

> "Damballah, may I (mention your own name) come out victorious in my dealing with (mention the person's name).

Work with the doll each day at the same hour for nine days. After the image is named and tagged, this should never change. No doll should be used for more than one person. If you wish to influence several persons, use a different doll for each one.

Add to your daily bath a spoonful or two of High John Conquering or Success Bath, and see what a difference there will be in your life in just five to seven days! After the bath, rub some Controlling Powder on the arms and around the shoulders.

Certain hours are more useful for various operations, and rituals concerned with power, influence and glory should be connected to the hours of the Sun. Therefore, burn your Attraction or Lucky

Planet Incense at the evening Sun hours which are:

Sunday	8:00 PM
Monday	5:00 PM or Midnight
Tuesday	9:00 PM
Wednesday	6:00 PM
Thursday	3:00 PM or 10:00 PM
Friday	8:00 PM
Saturday	4:00 PM or 11:00 PM

SO BE IT. . . . .

Other influential charms and talismans . . . .

A scarab design worn, or one of green jade carried, is reputed to make all dreams come true.

Great mystical powers are said to come to those who carry a Schemhamphoras No. 2 Seal from the Sixth and Seventh Books of Moses.

Take three pieces of ribbon, thread, or yarn—one red, one yellow, and one blue. Tie in each one three knots, repeating the name of the one you wish to do your bidding as you tie each one. Then bind all three pieces together and carry them or wear them on your person. The person you have bound in this manner will not be able to resist your wishes or commands.

War Powder, sprinkled on your body or around the room, is said to overcome feelings of animosity in others.

Schemhamphoras
2 Seal

FOR ONE WHOSE BUSINESS IS POOR

If Dame Fortune has stopped smiling on your endeavors, examine yourself to determine if your own deficiencies have caused your troubles. The God of Mammon has two heads and can speak good and evil at the same time. Pacify the gods so that the good face will be always toward you and your business.

Each and every day, before opening your store or shop, sprinkle a bit of Jinx Removing Salt in front of the door. Then sweep it or wash it away, being sure that none remains behind. Business Powder should then be placed on the threshold so that people will walk on or over it without noticing it is there. A trail of Gold or Silver Magnetic Sand sprinkled from the sidewalk or door all the way to the cash register, or money box, is helpful in many cases.

In a small red flannel bag, carry with you at all times a Seal of Good Fortune from the Sixth and Seventh Books of Moses which is reputed to bring much fortune and many blessings. Anoint your bag once every seven days with Success Oil.

An old legend for turning paper into money is to take thirteen pieces of paper cut to the size of money bills. On each one, write the following spell and sign your name.

I do not wish to gain control
of wealth for evil purposes.
I wish that I might have for me
rewards to match my virtues.

Hide these pieces around your shop so that customers may find them, but they should not be displayed in open view. It is alleged that anyone who touches one of these papers will be inclined to buy your products or use your services and these thirteen pieces of paper can turn into many times $13.00 before the day is over.

Be sure to use some Success Bath in a tub of warm water each evening. The merits of this bath may help you not only in your business efforts, but in the evening's activities as well.

Your customers should always be treated with due consideration and with honesty. Have the kindness of your heart showing on your countenance so that the customers will come to you and give you confidence and respect and they will go away and tell their friends about your sincerity and integrity.

SO BE IT. . . . .

SEAL OF FORTUNE

TO OVERCOME A BAD HABIT

Only good habits should be practiced, for a bad practice of one's own doing can prove a far greater enemy than any other outside influence from another person.

As an aid toward washing away malignant forces and encouraging helpful spirits to reach toward you, take a daily bath to purify oneself and add to this bath water a bit of Chinese Wash or a few Holy Herbs tied in a small bag.

At dusk each day, sit quietly and concentrate on the bad habit to be overcome. Think of the bad custom being defeated and fading away. Picture some of the benefits you may enjoy with the habit gone from your life.

Light some Helping Hand or Spiritual Good Luck Incense, and then a black candle, saying, "Here is that which holds me back. It is not good for me and well do I know it. It seems a mighty giant that is not to be conquered. Yet do I know that not to be so, for conquer it I will."

Then, light a white candle, saying "Here is my strength, here is my courage, here is my fortitude, here is my victory. Now is mine enemy surrounded. Now knows he not which way to turn. The battle doth begin, yet is the end well-known."

Bring into your mind the vision of the forces of good coming toward you, marching in on the enemy which is the bad habit. After a few moments of concentrating on this image, say quietly and reverently the following or a similar prayer:

Oh, Lord, make me stout of heart,
give me power to overcome,
drive the evil from me,
give me victory,
never desert me.

Extinguish both candles when your prayer is finished. Repeat the ritual each evening for three consecutive days. And for best results start the ceremony on the first Sunday after the next new moon.

Whenever you go out of the house, carry with you in your

pocket or purse, a small bag which contains a pair of lodestones, one of which is for repelling evil and the other for attracting good spirits, plus a Seal of Spirits or a Seal of Spiritual Assistance, either of which is designed for help from friendly forces.

Before retiring each evening, repeat Psalm 36 which is concerned with the wickedness of man, and then Psalm 35 which is a prayer for help.

Do these things with faith and constancy, and you cannot fail to triumph over the destructive forces at work within. Let not your heart be discouraged by temporary lapses, but persevere and the spirit of success will smile on you.

SO BE IT. . . . .

Additional charms, talismans, and amulets . . . .

A carbuncle, carried on one's person, is believed to increase one's self-confidence and ability to fight.

Some persons always carry a buckeye as a talisman for success.

An amethyst is alleged to bring the owner good luck, to cause peace of mind and calmness, and to protect against drunkenness.

Place a Little John Chew Root in a cup or glass of Water of Notre Dame and leave to soak overnight. This is said to bring success to any undertaking you attempt.

Controlling Oil rubbed on the temples is said to bring peace of mind to the unsettled and disturbed. Can also be used to anoint the piece of parchment on which you have written a situation or problem you wish to control.

TO PROMOTE PEACE IN THE HOME

Begin the ritual on your most favorable day. For those born under the sign of:

Leo or Capricorn. . . . . Monday
Cancer or Taurus. . . . . Tuesday
Pisces or Virgo. . . . . Wednesday
Aries or Libra . . . . Thursday
Sagittarius or Aquarius . . . . Friday
Scorpio or Gemini. . . . . .Saturday

Making sure that no one sees you or knows about it, sprinkle some Jinx Removing Salt or Powder at every corner of your home. Do this in the late evening hours, and the next morning wash it away with water or sweep it away with a broom.

To rid a home of evil spirits which may be inhabiting it, pour a bowl of fresh water to which you will add about two spoonsful of new salt. Take this bowl into every room of the home and breathe these words onto the water's surface, mentally visualizing–and this is most important–with all the faith, will, and imagination you can muster, a dim bluish light beginning to hover over it as you chant–

Water and earth, where you are cast,
No spell nor adverse purpose last,
Not in complete accord with me,
As my word, so mote it be!

When this is done, place the bowl outside and leave it. Do not pour the water out but let it disappear of itself.

Use two or three drops of Peace Oil in your daily bath, and after each bath anoint your forehead with this same oil.

Alternately use John the Conqueror and Helping Hand Incense. Burn one of these each day, and the vibrations within the place where this combination is used should become filled with harmony, love, understanding, and peace instead of friction, confusion, and disappointment.

A white candle should be used in the home, and the word "Peace" must be written nine times on a square of parchment and placed under the candle before it is lit for the first time.

There should be cheerfulness in your face, and no frown must be reflected on it. Keep evil or vindictive thoughts out of your mind, and peace and contentment will surely follow.

Psalm 139 should be prayed to increase and preserve love among married people. Psalm 140 is said to be a powerful means to remove growing hatred between man and wife. Psalm 137 prayed sincerely, it is believed, will root out of the heart the most inveterate hate, envy, and malice.

SO BE IT. . . . .

FOR PROSPERITY and BETTER FINANCIAL CONDITIONS

Prosperity is here for all to obtain if approached in a moral and ethical way, but it must be pursued with fortitude, tenacity, and patience.

Each morning on arising sprinkle a bit of Magnetic Sand, either gold or silver will do, in front of the door to your home, or across the doorway to your place of business. While you are doing this, pray earnestly and sincerely, in your own words as you feel, or as follows:

> O Lord, we are sorely tried in these days of want and need, yet we are trusting in Thee. Thou hast promised to open Thy hand to satisfy every living need. O Lord, in Thy mercy turn Thy face toward us and give us today that which we need to sustain our body and life. Take from us all anxious thoughts and worries, and fill our soul with peace, forgiving all our sins. O my Heavenly Father, Thy will be done. Amen.

In your daily bath, preferably taken in the morning hours, use one tablespoonful of Money Drawing or Success Bath. After the bath apply some Magnet Powder to the wrists and ankles.

Only Lucky Planet or Money Drawing Incense should be burned and this should be lighted at the Jupiter hours which are:

Sunday	6:00AM, 1:00 and 8:00 PM
Monday	3:00 and 10:00 AM, 5:00 and 12:00 PM
Tuesday	7:00 AM, 2:00 and 9:00 PM
Wednesday	4:00 and 11:00 AM, 6:00 PM
Thursday	1:00 and 8:00 AM, 3:00 and 10:00 PM
Friday	5:00 and 12:00 AM, 7:00 PM
Saturday	2:00 and 9:00 AM, 4:00 and 11:00 PM

Several of the Seals from the Sixth and Seventh Books of Moses are of value, and it is wise to carry one or more of these with you—Seal of Relief from Want, Seal of Treasures, and a Seal of Good Luck and Fortune.

Each day at sundown repeat Psalm 72.

Be sure to treat your customers with due consideration and with honesty, and always have the kindness of your heart showing on your face so that customers will come to you and give you confidence and respect.

Do not forget that all fortune obtained through the use of charms should be shared with those more unfortunate than yourself. If this is not done, your improved conditions will not last beyond two moons.

SO BE IT. . . . .

Additional charms which may be used . . . .

Legend says that a moonstone kept wrapped in yellow cloth brings good fortune.

Green candles are burned for money and for good luck. The amount of money needed can be written on a piece of white paper and placed beneath the candle before it is lighted.

A magnetic horseshoe can be carried to attract luck.

Magnetic lodestones, especially green ones, are lucky symbols. Carry a pair, one to repel evil and one to attract luck.

To increase your wealth, soak the gold part of marigolds in water for three days. Add a few more marigolds each day. After three days pour in a little red wine and a white feather. Keep this mixture in your window until you have the amount of money you need.

Sleep with some mistletoe at your feet and you will become adept at discovering treasure.

Fast Luck Powder, sprinkled around when a change of luck is needed, is said to work without fail. It should be used regularly to attract financial gains and new loves.

Some May Apple, carried around in the pocket, is said to be a protection against ever going broke.

A Southern John the Conqueror Root may be carried for luck and success in everything you undertake in life.

Spearmint, when crushed and added to any incense, is said to attract customers to a store, or renters to an empty house or apartment.

TO STOP GOSSIP OR SLANDER

It is often impossible to ascertain who is the instigator of the evil scandal or the nasty rumors that are hurting you. So it is suggested that you carry several small bits of Low John the Conqueror Root with you whenever you are out, and drop a piece of the root in front of the house of those you suspect of speaking against you. Should you meet any of these persons, drop the root in their path so they will walk over it as they leave your presence.

Each morning upon arising, repeat the 52nd Psalm sincerely and it will give you succor and courage. In your own home, you should use Helping Hand or Protection Incense. While the fumes are rising from it, stand in the center of the room looking towards the door so that evil thoughts will depart your home just as the fumes are slowly vanishing and leave you clear of all harmful vibrations. Light the incense at the Mars hours –

Sunday: 2 and 9 PM — Monday: 6 PM
Tuesday: 3 and 10 PM — Wednesday: 7 PM
Thursday: 4 and 11 PM — Friday: 1 and 9 PM
Saturday: 5 and 12 PM

Carry in your purse or pocket a Seal of Mephistophilis which is designed for conquering enemies, and anoint it with a drop of High Conquering Oil every third day. The High Conquering Oil can also be used to anoint your own body, particularly the wrists and earlobes so that you will feel no hurt nor hear any evil words being spoken against you.

Pour one teaspoonful of Uncrossing Bath in the water in which you bathe, and sprinkle some Confusion Powder or Get Away Powder in front of your home to confound those forces which may want to attack you and turn them back from where they came.

All your own actions should be above reproach. You will remember that you cannot stop gossip by gossiping, or criticising, or making derogatory remarks about any person.

All these things you will faithfully do so that the tongue of the viper will be everlastingly stilled, scandals and jealousies shall die, and in their place shall live only great joy and happiness.

SO BE IT.......................................

SEAL OF MEPHISTOPHILIS

Witches celebrating. Woodcut by Hans Weiditz.

TO WIN BACK A HUSBAND OR LOVER

Love and romance spells are more powerful when the moon is waxing, and certainly the ritual should begin during the Venus hours which are:

Sunday	2:00 and 9:00 AM	4:00 and 11:00 PM
Monday	6:00 AM	1:00 and 8:00 PM
Tuesday	3:00 and 10:00 AM	5:00 and 12:00 PM
Wednesday	7:00 AM	2:00 and 9:00 PM
Thursday	4:00 and 11:00 AM	6:00 PM
Friday	1:00 and 8:00 AM	3:00 and 10:00 PM
Saturday	5:00 and 12:00 AM	7:00 PM

So decide on a convenient starting hour and write your loved one a letter, sprinkling it with Attraction Oil before sending or mailing it. In composing your letter, express your own love for the loved one and avoid writing of any past mistakes or arguments. Express yourself as clearly as possible, and do not use words or phrases which may be misunderstood.

The Seven Knots Love Spell is designed to bind securely the love of whoever one desires to the operator of the ritual. If possible, place a photograph of the one you desire in front of you as you work and let your thoughts dwell on this person. Take a length of red ribbon or yarn, and tie seven knots in it, one each day, and in this order —1st knot in the middle of the yarn, 2nd knot a little to the right of the first, 3rd to the left of the first, 4th to the right of the second, 5th to the left of the third, 6th near the end of the material on the right, and the 7th near the left end of the material. As you tie each knot, repeat these words:

> "With this knot I tie your love and bind it firmly to mine. You will not be able to break it or loosen it. Your love will be completely mine and mine will be yours. We will stand together forever and nothing, nor any one, will be able to lessen, break, destroy, or interrupt our happiness."

Begin this ritual at the next full moon, and tie one knot each evening, repeating the words given. After the seventh day, and seventh knot, hide the love knots in a secret place. If necessary, the spell can be repeated on the next full moon with a new piece of ribbon or yarn.

During the time you are working on this spell, carry a Seal of Attraction with you at all times. It is designed for attracting others to you and may be of great benefit should you come in contact with the person you love.

Each time before you leave home to go out, apply Drawing Powder or Love Powder to your neck and inside the elbows. Some Attraction Oil can be used as a perfume also.

Write the name of the loved one seven times on a square of parchment (preferably in red ink) and place the paper under a red or pink candle which you should light each evening at the Venus hour.

Keep in your mind that love begets love, so give of yourself to the loved one, and let the sunshine of happiness enter your life.

SO BE IT. . . . .

Other love charms . . . .

To regain a lover who has left you, mix together some dragon's blood, sulphur, quicksilver, and saltpetre. Throw this mixture into a blazing fire, repeating the lover's name all the while. As these things burn, so should this person's heart burn for love of you.

San Cipriano Oil or Perfume is worn to force unfaithful mates to stop seeing other lovers.

Anoint the right toe of the one you desire with Controlling Powder and he, or she as the case may be, will soon be drawn toward you mad with love.

An Adam and Eve root, divided between two lovers, is said to bind them together.

Carry some vervain in a red flannel bag to attract a lover or new friendships.

Sprinkle couch grass under your bed to attract a new lover in seven days or less.

To keep a lover true to you always, grind fine some linden flowers and make them into a moist paste. Rub a bit on the head each evening before going to bed.

TO WIN FRIENDS AND POPULARITY

Proverbs XVII, 24: A man that hath friends must show himself friendly; and there is a friend that sticketh closer than a brother.

Daniel W. Hoyt from A Sermon in Rhyme says,

If you have a friend worth loving,
    Love him. Yes, and let him know
That you love him, ere life's evening
    Tinge his brow with sunset glow.
Why should good words ne'er be said
    Of a friend till he is dead?

These two quotations sum up the art of friendship and the secret to popularity. There is no need to be lonely and neglected and disliked. Examine your own feelings and attentions. Have you been remiss in maintaining your part of the relationship with others? Was it you perhaps who injured the other party even though it was unintentional?

To gain new friends, effort on your part must be made. Keep a cheerful smile on your countenance at all times, and make yourself attractive to others so that you will be noticed. As an aid to this objective, a daily bath is recommended and after the bath rub some Compelling Powder on the wrists, ankles, and throat.

When leaving the house, use only Cleopatra Oil as a perfume. This is a potent oil and should be used in very small amounts.

When washing your clothes, add two teaspoonsful of Lucky Bluing to the wash water. In your dresser drawers, place a Tonka Bean or two which gives off a pleasing aroma and sweetens the clothes you will wear. A bit of Lavender will accomplish the same purpose.

A pink or red candle should be lighted for a few minutes at sunset each evening. Place your candle in a wide flat dish or saucer and around the bottom of it, arrange three small stones or pebbles. You should mark each stone with the name or initials of the person it represents. When the candle is lit, and the wax drips down, notice which stone is touched first by the melted wax. This is the person you should concentrate on becoming friendly with. Take the time that same evening to write that person a friendly letter and arrange a meeting as soon as possible. See the results within a few weeks if not sooner.

In your home, burn Helping Hand or Lucky Planet Incense.

At all times, keep in mind that friendship is made up of love, good will, steadfastness, honesty, and kindness. You must offer all these qualities to another in order to have a true friendship. The one who can present these gifts to others will never lack for friends or popularity.

SO BE IT. . . . .

ROOTS AND HERBS

The origin of root and herb sorcery is unknown, but the ancient Romans, Greeks, Celts, Druids, Arabs, Egyptian Priests, and others all knew of the magical powers of roots, barks, herbs, plants, woods, and berries. Many herbs are mentioned in the Bible—and The Wise Men brought frankincense and myrrh to the newborn Jesus. Man has carried roots and herbs as amulets and talismans for protection from evil, and many believe they can heal, bring good fortune, arouse a lover, bring back a wandering husband or wife, and make wishes come true.

The legends of the plant sorcery abound in ancient folklore, regional superstitions, medieval grimoires, and numerous occult books. It should be remembered that there are many different spells for most herbs, and each root or herb can be used for various purposes. The same herbs may be mentioned by several authors as being used in divergent ways—to be carried, worn, buried, or made into tea —and for differing purposes—for good or evil, for protection or for hexing. The reader's use of all spells should depend on his own personal experimentation and the results received from the ritual and materials used.

This volume omits all impossible or ridiculous rituals which call for materials such as the right hand of a corpse, newt's blood, the eye of a basilisk, the heart of a screech owl, the tongue of a man, or an unborn infant's liver. Only those which require simple and available herbs and materials are included.

Herbs for MISCELLANEOUS PURPOSES

AGUE WEED-Burn to destroy an enemy's power to harm.

BAY LEAVES—Place in each corner of the room to avoid being hexed.

BROOM TOPS—Boil with salt and sprinkle to banish poltergeists.

BUCKTHORN—Tea made from this is said to remove warts.

COWSLIP FLOWERS—A bit under the front porch discourages visitors.

DANDELION—Bury at the northwest corner of home to bring favorable winds.

GRAVEL ROOT—Carry in the pocket when looking for a job.

JOE-PIE—Carry this so that you will be looked upon with favor by all persons.

KNOT WEED—Mix with soft wax and bury to destroy your problems.

LION'S TOOTH—Soak for six days and sprinkle on the seventh for year's luck.

POKE ROOT—Add to melted wax and throw into water to force an enemy to move away.

PRIMROSE—Sew into children's pillow to insure their respect and loyalty.

TRILLIUM—Money is attracted to the owner of this.

VALERIAN—Used as "graveyard dirt" in spells for evil purposes.

VANDAL ROOT—Burn with Black Arts Incense for hexing spells.

WOODRUFF—Carry in a leather bag for protection from all harm.

YELLOW DOCK ROOT—Steep into a tea and wash door knobs with the water to draw money or business into the premises.

YERBA SANTA—A holy herb carried for spiritual strength and blessings.

Herbs and Roots for BLACK MAGIC

BLACK MUSTARD SEED—To cause strife and stress in the life of someone you dislike, sprinkle some of these seeds in front of their door.

DEVIL'S BIT—Break some into small pieces and sprinkle it in front of the enemy's door. It is said that if this is done every seven days, the enemy may find that any evil sent out will not pass his door but will fall back upon his own head.

GRAPE VINE—Cut up in very small pieces and throw at a foe. This is said to cause eventual paralysis in those parts it hits.

KNOT GRASS—Use for casting extremely evil spells on an antagonist who has caused you serious harm. Combine this with melted black wax and a piece of paper on which you have inscribed the enemy's name. When this has hardened, burn it at night when the moon is dark.

LITTLE JOHN CHEW—This root when carried around in your pocket is said to reverse the effect of any hex and cause harm to the one who crossed you in the first place.

SKUNK CABBAGE—Take a bit and throw it in front of your enemy's house. Repeat this once every seventeen days to keep your foe in a crossed condition.

SLIPPERY ELM—Take an image or doll and tag it with the name of the one who is talking against you. Put the image (this can be a paper doll cut from a magazine, a photograph of the enemy, or an actual doll) in a small box and sprinkle it with Slippery Elm. Then stick a pin through the image's mouth, saying,

> "A blight be upon thy tongue,
> No more slander you will say of me."

Take the box and bury it as far as possible from your home. This will stop any gossip or quiet any slander against you from the person you have named in this spell.

SNAKE ROOT—To destroy another's love for you, mix some snake root with the person's nail clippings, hair, or worn clothing and burn it. That person will thereafter avoid you.

TORMENTILLA ROOT—Take a piece of paper (parchment if possible) and write the name of your enemy on it. Place some tormentilla root on the paper to cover your enemy's name and fold the paper securely so the writing does not show. Then cut a lemon half in two and place the paper between the lemon halves. Tie the lemon back together and place it in the sun. As the lemon dries up, so will the strength of your enemy decline.

VALERIAN—This foul smelling herb will surely cause your enemy much misery if you can arrange to sprinkle some in front of his path or doorway so that he, or she, will walk on it.

VETIVERT—This is to be used against one who has cursed or hexed the user. Line a small box with a black cloth and lay an image of the enemy on the cloth. A photograph, a paper cut out, or a doll of wax, straw, or cloth will do. Sprinkle the image with vetivert leaves while saying, "I bind thee to thine own evil. Upon your own head it shall be." Close the box and tie it with a cord, making nine knots. Take the box as far from your home as possible and bury it, or throw it into water. Walk away without looking back.

WITCHES GRASS—Grind some of this into a fine powder and use to sprinkle on voodoo dolls when you want to hex someone.

WORMWOOD—Take some butter or oil and heat it until it is melted and burned. Then add some wormwood and mix to make a sauce. Carry this sauce to some dark place where the sun never shines, as underneath the house or in a deep forest. Pour the sauce on the ground in a circular motion and say at the same time,

"Around and around, thy brains will turn,
Mixed and confused will they be,
Until the sun will this sauce burn,
No harm can thee send to me."

YARROW—Secure some of your victim's hair and mix it with some yarrow. Burn this at midnight on a night when there is no moon. As this mixture burns, say,

"As the hair of your head goes up in smoke,
May your evil affect me no more,
As the fire consumes the hair of your head,
May trials and troubles enter your door."

Herbs and Roots for GOOD LUCK—To gain wealth and success

It would be impossible to cover all the legendary roots and herbs used to bring good fortune, but some of the best known have been taken from various occult sources and are related as curiosa only.

ALFALFA—Kept in the home to protect its owner against poverty.

BASIL—An old voodoo law requries that one soak a heaping teaspoonful of basil in a pint of water. This water is then sprinkled in a place of business to attract money and success, and to keep away all evil.

BUCKEYE—Wrap a dollar bill around a whole buckeye and carry it in your pocket to attract money to yourself. Also, the buckeye is said to prevent rheumatism when worn about the neck.

CASCARA SAGRADA—This is used to help win court cases when brewed into a strong tea and sprinkled around the bed the night before an appearance.

CHAMOMILE—Brew and use as a hand wash before playing cards or gambling. Said to insure constant winning if used with regularity.

DRAGON'S BLOOD REED—Carry in a purse or pocket for good luck. When hidden under a mattress is said to cure impotency.

GALANGAL ROOT—One of these carried to court is said to make a jury feel favorably inclined toward you.

IRISH MOSS—Said to bring great good fortune to those who place a little under the rugs in their home.

JOB'S TEARS—Carry seven in your pocket for good luck.

JOHN THE CONQUEROR ROOT—Just before going out to play, gamblers boil this root in water and wash their hands in the water to enhance their chances of winning.

LOW JOHN ROOT—It is alleged that if one wraps money around this root the money will multiply and provide wealth for the one who carries it.

LITTLE JOHN—Place one in Water of Notre Dame and leave to soak overnight. This should bring luck in everything you attempt.

LUCKY HAND ROOT—This tiny hand-shaped root is said to convey good fortune and other benefits to whoever possesses it. Those roots which outline all five fingers are very scarce and highly prized.

MANDRAKE—Soak the root in wine every Friday and keep it wrapped in a red silk cloth. When carefully cared for, it is claimed to cause money left near it to double overnight. A whole root is extremely hard to obtain and is literally worth its weight in gold!

NUTMEG OF INDIA—To carry a whole nutmeg is a favorite with any who play games of chance. To make the nutmeg more powerful, bore a hole in one end of it, insert some quicksilver, and seal it with wax. Protect it by carrying in a red flannel bag.

QUEEN OF THE MEADOW—When added to the bath water, it is reputed to bring good luck in all new endeavors.

ROSEMARY—Place some under a pillow for luck.

SACRED BARK—Said to bring luck to the possessor who carries this.

SEA LETTUCE—A small bit kept in a bottle of alcohol on the window sill will insure good luck to all who live within the house.

SILVER LEAF—A potent good luck charm when kept in the home.

SNAKE ROOT—Voodooists believe that one should soak the root in a cup of boiling water for fifteen minutes. The water is then strained and the root thrown away. The liquid is put in a bottle and left for seven days. On the eighth day, it is rubbed all over the bottom of one's shoes. The voodoo legend is that a person so anointed will be led toward money, either to find it, win it, or gain it in some other manner.

SUMBUL ROOT—Legend says that this should be worn or carried near the heart to ward off diseases and bring good luck.

TONKA BEANS—Carry with you in a red flannel bag to attract good fortune and financial success.

VIOLETS—It is said that to sprinkle violets in the corners of your home will entice the good spirits to come and bring you many blessings. Violets are also said to give off healing vibrations in the event of illness in the house.

WONDER OF THE WORLD ROOT—Keeps all things favorable when placed in all corners of a house.

Roots and Herbs for HEALTH and LONG LIFE

Illness should be treated by a legal physician and his prescriptions and advice followed. None of the following legendary spells are recommended as treatment of any sickness or disease. They are related as curiosa only, and have been taken from various occult sources and ancient folklore or superstitions.

AFRICAN GINGER—Place under the pillow one sleeps on to cure a sore throat, and to protect against evil.

ASAFOETIDA—This is worn in a cloth around the neck to ward off colds and evil. Because it is so highly aromatic, it is said to be the incense of the Devil.

ASH TREE LEAVES—Place one tablespoonful of leaves in a bowl of water and leave it in the bedroom overnight while sleeping. In the morning it should be thrown away and renewed each night. This is alleged to prevent all illness and to keep one healthy.

BETONY—Strengthens the body when worn as an amulet. Also is a protection against evil spirits if sprinkled near all doors and windows.

CARAWAY SEED—Place some in a small red flannel bag and sew the bag shut with a white thread. Hide this in the crib or bed of a child to keep the young one free from illness or harm.

CORIANDER—The seeds are carried in a small bag as a charm against illness, disease, and headache.

DILL SEED—Tie some in a cloth and smell it to help cure hiccoughs.

DOG GRASS—Sprinkle all around the house to overcome depression. Do this for seven days and you will no longer despair.

EUCALYPTUS—Said to be an excellent protection against colds if stuffed into the pillow one sleeps on.

FENNEL SEED—To cure fits caused by witchcraft, wear around the neck, or carry in the pockets, some fennel seed tied in a paper on which you have written this:

CALLEN DAN DANT
DAN DANT CALLEN
DANT CALLEN DAN

This is said to remove any trembling arising from demoniacal possession.

HOLY HERB—This is used in the bath water for protection and for its healing power.

JOHN THE CONQUEROR ROOT—This is reputed to offset moods of depression and confusion when carried in the pocket.

LIFE EVERLASTING—This is kept in the home, or carried on the person, as a potent charm against both serious diseases and minor illness.

MASTERWORT—When sprinkled in the shoes, it is claimed to prevent weakness and tiredness. When mixed with an oil and rubbed on the neck, pains will be eased.

MUSTARD SEED—Carry with you at all times a few grains in a small bag or box, and a paper on which you have written these words, "Light, Beff, Cletemati, Adonai, Cleona, Flcrit." This is done to keep you from all injury.

QUINCE SEED—Protects one from all physical harm when a few of these are carried in a red flannel bag.

ROSE BUDS—Place these around sprains and bad bruises to quickly clear them up.

RUE—To relieve a headache, lie down and place some on the forehead. Wear some at night next to the heart to regain health from minor illnesses.

ROSEMARY—Carrying a bit of rosemary with you is said to improve both the mind and the memory.

SOLOMON'S SEAL—Each morning on arising, hold this in your left hand as you say,

"Strengthen my bones, this I pray,
Increase my breath, just for today,
Postpone all pain, and turn death away."

Then throw the Solomon's Seal over your right shoulder.

SUMBUL ROOT—Wear a piece over the heart to ward off all illnesses.

THYME—Burn in the home to attract good health for all occupants.

VALERIAN—This is placed in one's pillow to quiet the nerves and insure peaceful sleep.

VERVAIN—Worn as an amulet, vervain is noted for its healing powers in curing fevers and poisoning.

Roots and Herbs for LOVE and ATTRACTION

ADAM & EVE ROOT—Purportedly used to win the one you desire. They are used in pairs, or rather a root is divided between two persons. If a woman wishes to attract a man, she gives him one portion of the root and she keeps the other, each person carrying the root with them at all times. Husbands and wives can divide these roots and carry them to insure the fidelity of each other.

ALOES—Write the name of the one you desire on a small piece of paper, preferably on parchment and in Dove's Blood Ink. Then take three hairs from your head and lay them on the paper. As each one is placed, say,

"By the power of the great Diana,
By the strength of the Mighty Horned one,
Let all this of mine, all that of thine,
Be now and forevermore as one.
This boon I seek in the name of Diana."

Now fold the paper with the hairs inside and burn the paper to ashes. Mix the ashes with an equal amount of aloes and scatter this in equal parts toward the four points of the compass.

ASH TREE LEAVES—The occult uses are many—both to bless and curse. A few leaves on your person in a small bag are carried to keep one from drowning. A bit added to the bath acts as a skin softener. They can be carried to prevent witchcraft and the evil eye, as a love talisman to attract the opposite sex. Also reputed to have the power to mend a broken heart when worn.

CLOVES—Fill two small bags with cloves and suspend each on a leather thong. Give one necklace to a friend and wear the other. This will insure friendship between the two persons as long as the bags are worn.

CORN FLOWERS—Strife and discord will end, and harmony will enter the home where these are sprinkled.

DAMIANA—Let some soak in a glass of wine for three hours. Then sprinkle a small bit outside your front and back doors. Do this faithfully each day for twenty one days, and it is said that before long your wandering lover will return to you.

DILL SEED—Add a few grains to the bath water before going out to meet a person of the opposite sex. Said to make one irresistible.

DRAGON BLOOD REED—To bring back an unfaithful lover, wrap a piece of dragon's blood reed in a piece of paper on which you have written the name of the lover and throw it into a fire, saying,

"May he no pleasure or profit see,
Till he come back to me."

This reed is also said to cure impotency when placed under the mattress of the afflicted one. Good fortune will follow all who carry a piece of this.

HEARTSEASE—To soften a lover's heart, secret a bit in the sole of his or her shoes so they will walk on it unaware. After you have accomplished this, your advances will be welcomed.

KHUS KHUS—Add to bath water and it will make you attractive to the opposite sex. Also said to increase business.

LADIES' THUMB—Love is sure to enter the threshold where this is strewn.

LAUREL—Worn by brides to guarantee a long and happy union.

MARIGOLD—Add to the bath water to win respect and admiration from those you meet.

MARJORAM—This herb is attributed to Venus. To attract a husband, it is suggested that a woman put a little in the corners of each room of her home. It should be removed and renewed about once a month.

ORRIS ROOT—A love root, carried to attract the opposite sex and to make them love you dearly.

ROSEMARY—Give a special friend a bag filled with rosemary. This is supposed to induce warm feelings in another.

SCULLCAP—The woman who wears this insures her husband from other's charms.

SPIKENARD—Brew into a tea and wet the picture of a loved one with the water so they will never leave you.

SWEET BUGLE—Crush and sprinkle around your bedroom to attract new lovers and possibly marriage prospects.

YAW ROOT—Encourages romantic vibrations toward the carrier of this.

Herbs and Roots for POWER—Psychic, Spiritual, and Worldly

ACACIA—It is believed that the burning of this stimulates the psychic centers and messages from the spirit world can be more easily received and clearly understood.

ALTHEA—Aids in bringing forth the spirits when burned during any magical ceremony.

ANISE SEED—Aids greatly in the work of psychic phenomena when added to incense and burned.

BLADDERWRACK—Used in occult work, especially valuable when calling upon the sea spirits for favors or assistance.

BLOOD ROOT—Sprinkle some where the person you wish to gain power over will walk. The voodoo belief was that if tread upon, this person will act with kindness, respect, and will confer benefits on you. As you sprinkle the root, say these words,

O, friend to be, all evil retreat,
Find favor in me, when next we meet.

CALENDULA—Sprinkle a bit under the mattress to encourage prophetic dreams. Also, carry some in your pocket when appearing in court so that justice will smile favorably upon you and be lenient in your favor.

CELERY SEED—Used for increased concentration by mediums. Mix with incense and burn to heighten one's psychic powers.

DEVIL'S BIT—Also called Devil's Shoe String. There are many uses for this powerful root. Carried in the pocket at all times will protect against poison and bring luck to gamblers. Placed in the path of an enemy, he or she will have to face financial ruin. If it is cut up fine and added to a measure of whiskey and camphor, and then the mixture is rubbed on your hands, it is said to give either man or woman complete control over the opposite sex.

ELDER BARK—Write the name of the one you wish to control on paper (preferably on parchment in Dove's Blood Ink). Burn the paper in a metal dish. Then mix the ashes with Elder Bark in equal parts. Divide this mixture into seven equal parts. For seven nights, at midnight, bury one portion in a separate grave. By the seventh day, the person should be completely in your control.

GOAT'S LEAVES—If you are in conflict with another and it seems that the other person has control over you, take a few goat's leaves and boil them in an open pot for ten minutes. Let the water cool and strain. When the leaves are dry, wrap them in a paper on which you have written the situation you wish to influence and the name of the other person involved. Carry this on your person day and night for a week. By the end of the seventh day, the power will have begun to leave the other person and come to you.

HOLY HERB—Spinkle some on the grave of someone you wish to contact and that one will appear to you during the night in your dreams. Concentrate while steam is rising from the tea made of this and one's thoughts are carried to a higher spiritual plane so that spirits from the other world may appear.

HYSSOP—Soak a tablespoonful in one quart of water for twenty four hours, strain, and add the water to your bath water. This purification bath is recommended before meditation, ritual, or occult work. This is said to greatly increase one's clairvoyant powers.

LICORICE STICK—On a piece of paper, preferably on parchment and in Dove's Blood Ink, write the person's name whose mind you wish to change nine times. Now wrap this paper around a piece of licorice and tie it with a red thread or cord. In the dark of the night, bury it or hide it in or as near as possible to the home of the individual you wish to influence. A change in their attitude should become apparent in about three days.

MUGWORT—Said to aid toward astral projection if placed by the bed.

POLE CAT WEED—Should you have a neighbor you wish to dominate, a bit of this weed placed in front of their door every seventeen days will keep your foe in a crossed condition.

QUEEN OF THE MEADOW—When this is placed in water and soaked for seven days, and then added to one's bath water, it gives one the power to foresee the future.

SILVER LEAF—The ability to find lost or hidden treasure is granted to the person who burns this and follows the direction of the smoke.

Herbs and Roots for PROTECTION—Getting rid of jinxes, hexes, crossed conditions, and evil spirits.

AGUE WEED—This can be mixed with any incense and burned to break the power of a hex which has been placed on one.

ANGELICA—To prevent evil spirits from entering the home, sprinkle some at each corner of the house, saying each time,

"Spirits of the dark,
Begone from me,
Only spirits of light
Will I see."

BAY LEAVES—One in the corner of each room of a house is believed a protection for those who live there as well as the house itself. Carried in purse or pocket, it is reputed to be a protection against witchcraft.

BETONY—Wear as an amulet to strengthen the body and as a charm against evil spells. Sprinkle inside the home near all windows and doors for protection against wicked spirits.

BLADDERWRACK—To be carried by the traveler as a protection, especially when traveling by water.

BLOOD ROOT—Place on window sills and near doorways as a protection against hexes.

BOLDO LEAVES—Sprinkle around the house to ward off any evil.

CINQUEFOIL—Take an egg and cut a small hole in one end. Drain the contents and let the shell dry. Then stuff the shell with cinquefoil and reseal the hole with tape. As long as this egg is kept in the home, that house will be protected from all evil forces.

CLOVER—Soak one tablespoonful in one cup of vinegar for three days. Then strain and sprinkle the vinegar in each corner of every room. All alien spirits will leave the premises.

COMFREY ROOT—When travelling, place a bit of this in the bottom of all baggage. This will insure your safety on the trip.

DILL—Mixed with salt, this can be scattered about the house as a counterspell to witchcraft.

ELM BARK—To quiet slander against you, bury some in a box with a voodoo doll which has been tagged with the name of the person who is speaking adversely about you.

FIVE FINGER GRASS—Legend says that if this grass is hung over the bedstead, it will ward off any evil that a hand with five fingers could do. Or make a tea of it, using the water to wash the hands and forehead nine times. This washes away any hexes, jinxes, or curses which may be on one. Each segment of the leaf is said to possess a special power—love, luck, money, power, and wisdom.

GILEAD BUDS—Two of these buds are to be carried as a talisman against the Evil Eye. They are also believed a protection against other curses or hexes.

HOLY HERB—For a protective bath, add a bit to each tub of water.

MARJORAM—A charm used in defeating witchcraft for anyone who is in league with the devil cannot bear the odor. Place a bit in each room of the house and renew it once a month.

MINT—No witch or vampire will come close to the house which contains a jar of this.

MISTLETOE—When worn about the neck, it is said to keep away witches and witchcraft.

MONKSHOOD—Carry as a protection from devils and demons.

MULLEIN—Place under your pillow to keep away demons and nightmares. Carry some with you to keep away wild animals and enemies, and to give you courage.

PEARL MOSS—Sprinkle this across the doorway of the home, and only the good spirits may enter.

QUEEN OF THE MEADOW—Banishes ghosts from wherever this is kept.

SULPHUR—Also known as brimstone. Burn this at midnight, just outside your back door, to drive away all evil.

TRUMPET WEED—Sew into a red bag and wear as a protection from all injury.

WAHOO BARK—Boil some bark in one quart of water for ten minutes. Strain and use the water to sponge a person who is possessed. While sponging the victim, say "Wahoo" aloud nine times.

Roots and Herbs for WISHING and MAKING DREAMS COME TRUE

AFRICAN MOJO WISH BEAN–To make a secret wish come true, place two beans in your pocket or purse and carry them for three days. Concentrate on your wish, and on the fourth day, throw the beans into moving water–a stream, river, or ocean. Wait seven days and the wish should have come true.

CALENDULA–Sprinkle dried bits of this flower under the bed. Makes all dreams come true, and protects the sleeper from evil.

CLOVES–Hold some cloves tight in the hand while thinking of a friend or lover is said to make them do your every bidding.

DANDELION–Sew tightly in a red flannel bag and wear around the neck to make wishes come true.

HUCKLEBERRY LEAVES–Burn in the bedroom before going to sleep to make all dreams come true in seven days.

JOB'S TEARS–As you count out seven seeds, concentrate on a wish you have in mind. Carry these seven seeds with you at all times for seven days, and your wish should have come true before the week is gone.

LAVENDER–Place some lavender under your pillow just before retiring and think about your wish. If you dream about anything at all connected with the wish, this means that the wish will come true. If you have no dream, or dream about other matters, the wish will not come true.

LOTUS ROOT–Mark one side of the root "yes" and the other side "no." Then make your wish, or ask a question and toss the root into the air. Whichever side lands up, this will be the answer to your question or whether your wish will come true.

PEONY–Write your wish on a piece of paper and sprinkle on it a bit of peony. Roll the paper up and seal it, preferably with melted red wax from a candle. Hide it in your home as you repeat these words,

> "Grant me today a wish,
> A large wish, a small wish,
> A tiny wish, a big wish.
> Growing here and growing there,

Growing slowly everywhere.
Grant me my wish so that I may rejoice."

Every third day, change the hiding place of your amulet, repeating the incantation given. After your wish has been granted, destroy the paper and peony by burning.

QUEEN ELIZABETH ROOT—Tie a piece of string around a root and let it hang down about ten or twelve inches. Use this as a pendulum for answers to questions you wish answered. Hold the string between thumb and forefinger and rest the elbow firmly on a table. Ask the question aloud or in the mind. If the root swings as a pendulum from right to left, the answer is "yes." If the root swings to and away from the person questioning, the answer is "no."

ROSE BUDS—Gently separate a rose bud and count the leaves as you go. If there are an even number of leaves, your secret wish will come true. If there are an uneven number of leaves, your wish will not come true.

SANDALWOOD—It is said that the burning of this as an incense will aid in bringing about the fulfillment of one's secret wish. As you light the incense, say, "Adonai, Elohim, Elohim, Adonai."

SPEARMINT—Write your wish on a piece of paper (preferably on parchment and in Dove's Blood Ink). Wrap the wish, along with a few spearmint leaves, in a red cloth and sew it up securely with red thread. Keep this in a safe and secret place, and, by the time the scent is gone from the spearmint leaves your wish should have come true. If it has not, it probably will not for a long time to come.

Macbeth and the three witches (Act IV, Scene i). From N. Rowe's first illustrated edition of *William Shakespeare's Workes*, printed by Tonson, London, 1709.